Attic of Stars
Poetry

Owl Willows

Dedications

For Grammie with much love
who always told me to write something interesting

***

In loving memory of my father,
Anthony Maulucci
1948--2018

Forever I feel your presence,
knowing you are here.
You are the ocean, the sky
the moon, stars, and sun.
You are the seasons, the laughter,
and the light which will always live within us.

Forward

The poems in this book were written over the course of a few years, and they explore both sadness and joy that we experience while on Earth, the thoughts and feelings about death of oneself and the passing of ones we love. I feel as though we spend much of our human existence ruminating and worrying about death and the afterlife, so some of this poems celebrate life.
Each of us have different beliefs and experiences which make our world a rich place to live, due to such diversity. My poems celebrate Earth and all of nature, and also deal with a multitude of emotions akin to the human experience,
These poems are about our life journeys, dreams, and loving those who pass on. They are about allowing ourselves to feel all emotions and grow through obstacles and challenges, including losing loved ones dear to us.

Some of the poems in this book are about reaching our goals, while two very special ones are fantasy. I have wanted to share my poetry with readers for a long time with hope that I can reach someone who may have gone through similar experiences. In my time here, I have found that whatever else there is, love is the most fundamental part of and reason for our existence.

Every day that I pass beneath the trees and look up into the sky, I hope that Dad and other loved ones are always with me, for my heart is always with you.

Dad, Remembered and Remembered

While I remain on this Earth without you
I know you in the rain, I know you in the wind

and ocean. You are the sunset which catches fire
in the brilliance of The Universe.

Mistakes we both made in the past were laid before
us, and cast aside. Unresolved issues are dissolved
and all that remains--is love.

Love for all of the times you held my hand, love for
the when I listened to your voice read stories, love
for the years we had together.

Dad, you are cherished and never forgotten.
You are remembered and remembered
by all of us from sunset to sunrise

I didn't know that our last hug
would be final
As the years passed. I knew it would be.

My hope is that in the tranquil peace
which I know surrounds you now
is that you see us in nothing but
understanding and love

***
I remember and remember how you loved
West Side Story

how you always dressed so well
the warmth of your hugs, and the style of
your paintings.

Then there were the smaller things,
but not less important all the same.
You loved chocolate cake
and always illustrated my birthday cards
making sure to include the things I loved.

You loved the Beatles, and so did I.
You were so sad when John Lennon died.
At one point, you even had his cigarette butt
but Grandma threw it away, not knowing.
***
Although times of darkness did exist
the good outnumbered the bad
and you were one of the dearest people I ever knew

I wish that you had known me later towards the end
Wish that you had told us that you were going to pass
With all that I know of the spirit world and in my own
heart
You are always be my side
***
When I walk into a museum or a library
I always think of you

Through you I discovered my favorite things.

When I visit the aquarium I like to watch the aquatic
animals
swim peacefully, and I think you must
enjoy this as I do.
We always loved the quiet so
This busy world, just not for us.

The Weather is Finally Changing

The weather is finally changing
and my heart has long missed the autumnal
wind and rain
I met with it today after so long,
as it brushed through
my hair to say hello
The wind cooled my quaking heart,
torrid after summer's hell
to take my hand and lead me into
a world of rain and willows
Long had this world seemed so far away
Yet as I passed beneath rain clouds

and into my favorite cemetery
the fiery trees remembered me.

It was the crows who sang their
old songs on stones from long ago
My heart they recalled
for even though my body had aged another year
my love never changed
Even though someday I will fade like the sunset
turns to night
like summer into autumn
into winter

The weather is finally changing
bringing hope and days to make memories
so dear.
Each year is a gift, so never shed a tear.

Coastal Cemetery Trees

The Earth sinks into the ground
it is tired, time for slumber.
Its last golden rays disappear into the autumn Earth
while my sneakers walk around the graves
marking time.
Someday I will be there, beneath the Earth
or in a Mausoleum,
but I will really be out there
beyond the air.

The trees are old ladies hands
Stretched across the sky
This is my home,
not beneath the harsh Midwestern sun,
but being rained on,
 feeling cold, and reading books of old.

This coastal cemetery has known me
intimately, like a friend
who I introduced to other friends.
They all thought it was beautiful
that it was pleasantly spooky and gothic.
But wasn't I afraid to walk all alone?

I took comfort in the rain.
It whispered to me, and
 fell on my hair and clothes
The coastal cemetery was my most understanding friend
for many years,
only I sense all the magic that comes from
Its Earth that covers bodies,
Some freshly buried and others skeletons with bits of flesh.
They listened to the worries of my heart
And were with me to watch the sunset skies.
Never will I forget such enchantment as spent wandering
through
its courtyards and graves.
I hope that it does not forget me.

Attic of Stars

When you passed into our lives
You became our loves.
Two furry cats--one black, and one striped
With little paws that loved to run about the house
up and down stairs
Especially at night

When you passed out of our lives
I wished I had been there, yet I never stopped
loving you, cherishing you as the first time we found
you at the Humane Society

I hope that you reached the attic of stars
where I like to think you are together in
an environment swathed in enough darkness
for cat naps and stars to remember the lights
of our Christmas trees
the candles of our dinners
and most importantly, our love

For love is light
Love is never ending

I wish an attic full of stars for you
With a couch of soft blankets
piles and piles of books to read
with stars to light the darkest nights
and a window so you can watch birds
to your heart's content.

I wish endless happy dreams as you
sleep in each other's arms
dreams of far away planets and fish
memories of us, the family of four who loves you

I wish an infinity of lazy nights as stars float
through the open attic space
as you try to catch them

I hope that you go on adventures, and always stay
together
Within a cat's heart is mystery, is chaos, is love.

He took care of you until the very end, and she always
watched out for you
While you live in our hearts forever

I wish a symphony of stars for you.

Reflections of Many Rainy Days

The rain puddles at my feet and I stare through it as a portal.

It is the only physical connection between here and home,
The beautifully romantic dreariness that only a pluviophile
could love
And it both ignites hope and the longing sadness that tugs
on my sleeves and
follows me everywhere I go

The rain connects me to memories and I feel as if I am
Still there, as angel feathers watching and waiting
For us all to be reunited in the sky
As if I could be part of the soil that feeds the trees
Beneath my beloved New England sky

Rain melodies, take me back to the willows
to the old pear tree with rotten fruit
Only to where the ocean meets with low clouds of the sky
And I can feel my father's left over presence

As my mother sets my mittens on the radiator
My imagination climbs the walls. All is silent and stationary
before all the yarping of technology, life is private museum
solitude
and my heart is terribly full.

It is now that I am more lost than ever
Find me a warm sweater so I can wear it
Inside out, because that is how it feels inside
To stay alive.

I spend so much time being okay, and the rainy days

are when I try to heal
There are so many things that I try to forget
And all I want to do is crawl inside
As hours pass into days, just try to remember all the good
things
Instead

That is when I go walking, walking in the rain
Past graves of people in the sky
And I know
It's okay
For things must happen as they will

Starlight of the Darkest Nights

A darkened night sat atop New England's skyline,
as a never ending backdrop to the living inhabitants
on Earth and other planets.
When I left, the night lasted years.

While I was away, the comforting rain clouds fell away
and the darkened sky came out to play.

Where I had to stay, the darkness was
within me everyday, but it was the starlight that gave me
hope.
When trapped inside this reality so dark, I could not see my
hands, and
although there was no water, just trees and land, I felt like I
was drowning

To look into the sky brought me despair, for I knew that
at home, Eastern Standard Time was the same
and everyone created art without me,
how my family missed me,
my childhood town only a memory,
all the places we went and things said
seemed lost forever.

My heart fell, and it rained so hard
that I could not see how to help myself,
so I wandered without seeing in a world
of utter darkness and despair.

There was a very persistent little star who followed
me,
he told me that no matter what he loved me
it was going to be okay.
On the wind, I heard the voice of the Universe
reminding me that I all of the power I needed was inside.

When I began to believe again that when we visualize,
we can create anything, the entire sky lit up with more stars

than I imagine existed.
I love you, and The Universe does too, said the little star.
And I cupped him in my hand, as we crossed the ragged
valley of rocks
I knew that we were on our way home, and that things
would be okay
I just had to trust, believe, and receive.

The more I believed and knew in my heart, that what I
desired greatly
to be true,
the more I cast aside things that made me sad, The Universe
co-created
my new reality.

My journey was not only through Earth and sky, but within
heart and mind.
I am home, the ocean at my feet, and its mist in my hair.
I whispered every night before falling asleep in the Midwest.
No matter how dreadful the day, or the sadness, I told
myself to love and to believe.
I practiced joy, and believing without seeing. All
throughout, my star kept me company
and filled my heart with love.

Time passed and the weather changed, children were born,
persons returned to the
Sky, and welcomed by The Universe
The cycle of life continued, and as I looked into the sunsets
and gray afternoon clouds that I could now see,
I knew that up there in The Universe, my dream was

nurtured and true.

We filled our days, my star and I, with art and joy
with love and bravery,
we practiced well our happiness, acted as if
while doing what we loved, by nurturing animals and
enjoying the rain
everyday was a new adventure, and we let nothing lead us
astray.

One day, when I least expected it, The Universe had it all
arranged.
It was time to pass from this land, to go home to the ocean
beneath
the greatest array of stars that led the way.
They brought us all the way home, they brought tears to my
eyes.
There we stood in Maine, my star and I.

Our great land of sleepy rain clouds and small coastal towns
waited for us.
Dreary trees over ancient cemeteries welcomed us, and so
we danced amongst them beneath the celestial sky,
the moon and stars.
All the world was love, and we were dazzled.
We understood that sometimes, the darkest night is before
the dawn.
But the only answer is true joy and love.

Earth Day Poem

Wet soil as the rain falls down
through the orange leaves
and onto the ground

Earth, you gave us a place to call home
Beneath cloudy storms and starlight skies,
Through rolling thunder we have heard your cries

Our people have been cruel
Abused Mother Earth and her animals
For profit and greed
On Earth Day
And everyday we stand
So you do not fall

Today and always we recycle
Reminding each other to do it
Without falter
Together as a people we revere the rain,
Rivers, mountains, valleys, and trees
Outstretched to the never ending horizon
That sees all the years before we do

Your autumns grow large pumpkins
For our pies
Winters bring snow and rosy cheeked children.
In spring your trees watch over people relaxing in the park,
And bookworms like me reading beneath trees

In all of the summers of my childhood have left me
memories
Of my grandmother, Misty, and me.

Without our Earth
We would be homeless
Cast aside into the cold Universe
Without our Earth
I would never be able to watch my rainy New England sky
Through the skeletal boughs of old trees
Or watch the waves crash into rocks and sand,
Or build a home
With my partner

Like the Universe
The Earth has given us all so much

Today and always we give back
To the Earth, Sky, and Stars
We work towards ending pollution
Recycling whenever we can
Through teaching others, we can spread the word
About what it means to love Earth and all who inhabit it

Mountains Between

Blue gray windows look outside
at trees that are not mine,
at a sky I do not recognize.

Loneliness I feel, for you are not real

The windows show a rain filled sky that is endlessly peaceful
I try to find a friendly face, but you are always in the back of
my mind

There is cheer in the butterflies and flowers from the
ground
The Universe tries to guide me through
But where are you, and why did you tread so far?

The city lights at night make me feel so lonely
because you have no idea where I am, and you don't care.
 All I can think of now, is how Hartford looked in the dark
when you and mom held me close.

Still I always worried I'd be abandoned and left behind
I hope that you still love me like I do
and I want to tell you, how very much I love you.
There are mountains between us and I can't see a thing
You seem such a mystery, like Father Time with a beard like
the sky
Dad, where are you?

It's not always about location for I can pin you on a map, to
a place
I'll never go.
It's more the emotional distance.
I want to hug you, and tell you about all the things I create,
and why I'm sad

Every day I think of you

as the sun rises and falls.
You haven't seen me and it hurts to see other fathers
as I become part of other families but not my own.

You have left so much behind you.
All of the rainy hours spent at The Book Barn
and having adventures together.
The enormous mansion and stoney lighthouse at Avery
Point
chase through my mind hauntingly, because you loved and
showed us these things.

They are now a part of me as are you,
all that I am of you with inventions of my own make
me a creative loner, but who am I and who are you?
For my old life with you feels like fiction now.

The Secret of Rose Garden Park
From my novel, The Paperback Write of Central Park

Sunlight sleeps in the earthen soil, until the sun urges it
awake
To rise above the secret park
In hopes that visitors have found their way back home
Once a usual park, with lamp post lined pathways and cozy
Wooden benches for reading, it has been forgotten
And haunted by memories only the trees remember
Trees have long memories and sensitive hearts

Grass hasn't grown in years, it is frozen over with morning
dew
The afternoons never came to warm it up
Because the park is a secret, hidden away
And out of balance.
Only morning and night exist here, so it is a very cold place

To get into the actual garden
You must pass under the thorn rose archways

And climb the stone steps to the abandoned courtyard
Sodden with beautiful fountains that have been dried up for
years

Here grass grows, animals prowl and life almost seems
normal
But it has been waiting in transfixed solitary
Still
Except for the wind blowing through the empty spaces in
trees
The motionless pond, and the exquisite thorny rose garden
Tucked away behind a door to tomorrow that opens into
yesterday

The Forgotten Rose of New England
From my novel, The Paperback Writer of Central Park
Trees nestled in a corner of the universe
to spread their wings and grow
They were willows, oaks, and pines
New England trees
Watchful of the souls loved by the universe
Through the trees, rain falls as it does every day
Cool air surrounds this beautiful , esoteric land
Old castles and sprawling Victorians lay undisturbed by time
In the town of The Rose, there is only here and now
Forever and ever, its own Nirvana
The forgotten Rose lies hidden in a Mystic Cottage
And behind a door in a very lost garden that
Only the finest souls may open.
The dearest of heart and purest of intention will ever and
only
Experience the beauty of the Rose
They will have all the time in the universe
To behold the Rose's natural beauty
Hearts stop and clocks fail to tick in the forgotten town
Of the Rose
Only the spirit may enter, taking whatever form it wishes
Never will the heart mourn, because nothing is lost within
The Rose
Here the streets unfold that their hearts always knew
Underneath the trees that watched them as children
Now soulmates they kiss, and hold hands and hearts
They were led through by the wizard
Who observes and advises
Guides and works his magic for the

God and Goddess of nature
They will remember childhood afternoons
Spent in the rain
Walking through the cemetery for a sense of solitary
Feeling the ever cool air on their skin and hair
Together with nature, apart from their dichotomy with
other people

In the world of The Forgotten Rose, there are lazy quiet
days
Of reading novels of fantasy, mystery, and thrilling tales of
mysticism
There is always the rain, it lulls the inhabitants of this little
town to sleep
And in a waking state, it creates constant peace
The very energy they felt holds their living dreamscape
together
They are River and Elizabeth, the two souls destined to rule
the peaceful
Land of The Forgotten Rose
The wizard walks with his ancient cat, Dathatel
As the curator of town, and all of its memories
Together, the four beings must protect and preserve this
gentle world
Of forever rain and tree spirits

Within Us

Within me is the harmony of the sea
and the whispers of my voice, all the thoughts and poems
That are mine.

Though travels are long
my heart lies with the rain and stormy skies,
never will I forget Father's orange lounge chair
library movies, or mother reading to me.

Within me is the quiet eccentric nature of the wind
Hailing from the starlit skies
Inside I am bright, my soul a thousand colors and my heart,
My heart beats for home

Within me is a unique soul of childlike reforms
and klutzy tendencies, but I'm the one
who understands me
I'm the starlight of the sea
I am brave, and look beyond society's box.
When he holds me I know that things will turn around.

It's okay to cry, but if you tear down the walls
You'll find The Universe on the other side
If you give up, you only have to look into a sunset
sky to see all the magic there

All of us have beauty in our step, so let us walk with grace
Use it to help others and ourselves to reach our dreams
For within me is the ocean that stretches as far as the eye can
see
Around me is the love of others, and The Universe.

Within me is great wonderment and admiration for all
that nature is.
Someday we shall all return,
as spirits we will embrace
as spirits we will forgive
and we will be together, as the great ocean spans on forever,

just like time.

Tapestry of Nature's Love

The sky ran down the windows in cool
droplets of hope,
all of which make up the ocean, fill my heart and follow
me through memories.

Gardens below tapestry the castle grounds,
and above is a sky of planets and stars,
without pollution or pain, this is the world
my heart longs for.

I love you, and I know that we must part for now
but in spirit, we will meet again.
The wind shall bring us together in the night of stars,
calming blue memories will drift through The Universe as
our spirits
do.

Love will lift us up, and we will meet with each other as the rain cleanses
old sadness from our souls.

On New England evenings, sunsets melt into the street like fallen
ice cream cones,
forever I will be a little girl, and I will bring all of those together who love me,
even if they hurt me,
for all eventually will be okay.

As the wind coasts along the deep dark waters, and waves devour
lighthouses, we slept in the lantern room to escape in dreams
to dance through the Universe,
and throughout it existed ponds so clear, you could see straight to the bottom.
As swans glided across delicately,
we realize,
that all of our Earth-bound fears have no residency here

Clouds passed by our historic neighborhood
And down came the rain on Penny Lane, blanketing me in daydreams
of mysterious far away castles, while feeding gardens all down the street.
Dearest rain, my constant friend and reading companion.

My heart runs over when lightning streaks across the sky,
and I feel connected
to a magic that exists within nature and each of us,
our gift from The Universe.
It is our life purpose to feel joy and give to others.
Beneath the tapestry of rain, or stars, of storms
we must live our lives, sorting through puzzling events,
and caring for beings of all shape, creed, and diversity.
for all is love, and all will be okay

As the moon regulates the ocean's waves,
and our friend the sun greets us at the beginning and end of
every day,
as it sets, it leaves us with a tapestry of love, of fiery red and
orange,
or of soothing blue and indigo.

For all is love, and all will be okay.

Haunted

Willows covered their cabin
hid the tangled garden
and all of their secrets

The rain fell in splinters against the roof
and it was The Universe she saw in The Earth
Sometimes she remembered yesterday

She stopped being afraid
They were only shadows and they couldn't
hurt her
The ghosts showed up in her attic
 but they only wanted to remind her
what the veil made her forget
That was why she liked hanging around the graveyard,
she missed what was beyond the horizon

But it was pretty here too on Earth
Especially when the sun woke up
the New England trees
And when it went to sleep

it left watercolors in the sky

She loved her parents even
If they didn't understand her
She just didn't know why she had come here
Why had she chosen to come back,
and where was he

They were supposed to meet
but where
She'd float around until then
Like the ghosts in her house
who called her name

Years later when she peered through the
cabin windows at the blue willows
She thought she heard her name on the wind
It was the ghost in the mirror
It was the grandfather clock in the hall

When the light bulb exploded she knew
it was her father come back again
and the fear dissolved once more
She could never be afraid
when so loved.

Heart Map

I did care,
But you never believed in me
I tried to shine brightly
like the stars across the night
our map homewards
but from your view,
I was perpetually unable to reach them

Somehow, I feel less loved
for my shortcomings
You weren't ever able to see me shine
before you slipped into eternal sleep
we ran out of time

You were there for my first breath
why couldn't I have been there for your last
why didn't you ever come home

The stars will guide you now
eternal rest keep you
You live within our hearts, in love

I always meant well
and tried
But I was always so lost
I tried to shine brightly
while you were here,
but I will reach the stars

Visit her website:
https://dragonspirit1989.wixsite.com/owlwillows